Teaching with Objects

First in the Series:
TREASURY OF CLASSROOM, FAMILY AND PARTY FUN

BY ALMA HEATON

Illustrations by Mary Adams

Bookcraft
Salt Lake City, Utah

COPYRIGHT © 1971 BY
BOOKCRAFT, INC.

16 17 18 19 20   89 88 87 86 85

Lithographed in the United States of America
PUBLISHERS PRESS
Salt Lake City, Utah

PREFACE

This book is the first in a series entitled **Treasury of Classroom, Family and Party Fun,** which combines learning with fun. Some of the books will offer games, stunts, puzzles and other activities by which the teacher, whether in home or classroom, can interest and intrigue the participants and thus stimulate them to learn and grow in the gospel. Some books in the series will feature solely entertainment items.

This first book, **Teaching with Objects,** contains nearly sixty object lessons. Jesus Christ, the greatest teacher, used object lessons in setting forth gospel principles. It is clear that we gain the greater percentage of all our knowledge through the use of the eyes. There are good reasons, then, why you should add object lessons to your classroom techniques.

There are three basic uses for the object lesson in the classroom or in family home evening:

1. As a **springboard** into a lesson, using the object to stimulate interest, impressively introduce a concept, or emphasize a problem.

2. As the **framework** for a presentation, using the object as the foundation for the material to be discussed. Object lessons are excellent for illustration and clarification.

3. As a **clincher,** to summarize a lesson and leave a memorable impression.

Following are suggestions to be remembered when selecting objects for the lessons:

1. Use objects which are clearly visible. Sometimes an enlarged model is needed, at other times a reduced model.

2. A valuable but little used resource is historical relics—pioneer clothing or household items, handmade nails, soil from historical places, Indian relics, old firearms, pioneer handicraft, and so on.

3. The object is only a means to an end—don't make it so unusual that it is remembered while the application is forgotten.

4. Use a variety of familiar objects, but limit the number for clarity. Never use the same object to represent more than one idea before the same students.

5. Use uncomplicated objects so that you can readily maintain eye contact, and student interest is not lost in a jumble of equipment and words. Object lessons are to be short and to the point.

6. Look for ways of involving the students. For example, seek an appropriate scripture that can be memorized to go along with the object lesson.

ACKNOWLEDGMENTS

Deep appreciation is extended to Sharon Atkins for her enthusiasm and help in compiling this set of books. Sharon has spent many hours in sorting hundreds of pages of material handed to me by students in my classes. As a result of her efforts the choicest items have been gleaned for these books.

I want to acknowledge not only their helpful suggestions but also the hours of work that my wife Marie and children Randel, Hal, Rochelle and Debra have spent on this material. They have given up many hours that could have been spent together in family recreation.

Grateful acknowledgment also goes to Mary Adams for the interpretive art work done in each of the books. All that was necessary for the art creations was a suggestion, and Mary's imagination and talent would do the rest.

Thanks go to JoAnn Leemaster for suggestions, and for editing and rewriting; also to Marilyn Miller and to Mr. and Mrs. Randy Collett for editing and rewriting.

CONTENTS

Appearance of Evil	1
Application of the Gospel	2
Appraisal of Others	3
Appreciation for Others	4
Brotherhood	5
Character	6
Chastity	7
Church Standards	8
Conformity	9
Eternal Life	10
Eternal Marriage	11
Evolution	12
Faith	13
Feelings	14
Goals	15-16
Godhead	17
Gospel Enrichment	18
Gossip	19
Holy Ghost	20
Honesty	21
Influence	22
Judgment	23
Knowledge	24
Light of the Gospel	25
Living the Gospel	26
Obedience	27
Participation	28

vi   Contents

Presentation	29
Priesthood	30
Problems	31
Repentance	32-34
Restrictions	35
Satan	36
Scriptures	37
Seeing Isn't Always Believing	38
Self-Discipline	39
Self-Improvement	40
Service	41
Sharing the Gospel	42
Sin Clouds the View	43
Social Pressures	44
Spirit of the Lord	45
Strength	46
Strong Physical Body	47
Talents	48
Teamwork	49
Temptations	50
Testimony	51-52
Three Degrees of Glory	53
Time for Seasoning	54
Tithing	55
Wealth	56
Word of Wisdom	57
Unity	58

APPEARANCE OF EVIL

Objective: To stress avoidance of the appearance of evil.

Material needed:

1. A piece of chalk about two inches long.

Presentation:

1. Have a member of the class hold the piece of chalk between his middle and index fingers.
2. Ask the class what the example reminds them of.

Lesson Application:

1. Even though the chalk is not a cigarette, others might think it was.
2. We should avoid the very appearance of evil so that our reputation remains unblemished.

APPLICATION OF THE GOSPEL

Objective: To show that the gospel is of no use unless applied in our lives.

Material Needed:

1. Two washed, raw fruits or vegetables
2. String, or other fasteners, to tie food to your person

Presentation:

1. Hang the fruits or vegetables on your person where they can be seen.
2. Explain that while the food may be good it will be of little use unless it is eaten and thereby becomes a part of the body.

Lesson Application:

1. Religion must be digested in order to nourish the spirit.

Teaching with Objects 3

APPRAISAL OF OTHERS

Objective: To show that we should look deeper than outward appearances in appraising someone's worth.

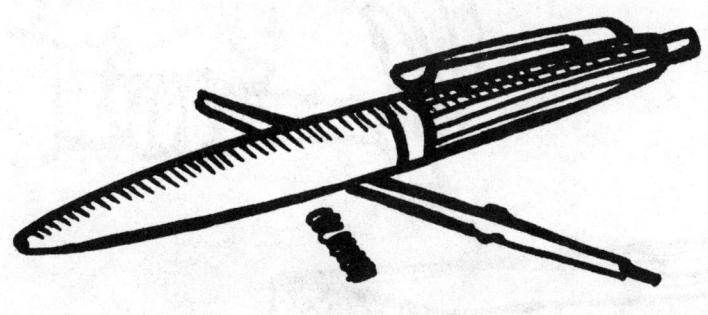

Material Needed:

1. A ball-point pen

Presentation:

1. Show the group a ball-point pen.
2. Then take it apart and remove the inside parts. Reassemble the outer portions.
3. The pen will look the same but will not write.

Lesson Application:

1. Don't judge people from outward appearances but look deeper for their true worth.

APPRECIATION FOR OTHERS

Objective: To stress that we need to show appreciation for the things others do for us.

Material Needed:
1. A small board
2. A hammer
3. A nail which is slightly bent in the middle

Presentation:
1. Show the class the bent nail.
2. Now try to pound the nail into the board. Explain that it will not go and only bends more.
3. Give the nail a "pat on the back" and straighten it.
4. Now it works perfectly.

Lesson Application:
1. Like the nail, people are sometimes reluctant to do their jobs.
2. If given a "pat on the back" and shown a little appreciation, these same people will work much better.
3. Like nails, people sometimes get bent out of shape and need to be coaxed back into shape.

Teaching with Objects 5

BROTHERHOOD

Objective: To show that we are all children of our Father in heaven.

Material Needed:
1. Paper
2. Scissors

Presentation:
1. Fold a piece of paper in wide folds, accordion style.
2. Starting at one of the folded edges, cut out half of the form of a figure, such as a boy or girl.
3. Be careful not to cut into either of the folded edges except at the head and feet of the side you started with.
4. Unfold the figure once to show the whole figure.
5. Ask the class how many figures you have cut. One? Several?
6. Now unfold the whole string. The figures will be holding hands if the paper has been cut correctly.

Lesson Application:
1. All of the people in the world are children of our Father in heaven. We are all made in his image and from the same mold. Thus we should accept all races and creeds as our brothers and sisters.
2. A missionary may convert one person to the gospel. This person comes in contact with many other people. If they really love their friends, they will take them by the hand to church. Thus one baptism may lead to many.

CHARACTER

Objective: To show that we make a record of our character each day.

Material Needed:

1. Tape recorder with tape OR shorthand notebook and pen

Presentation:

1. Ask a student to come up and express his thoughts or convictions on some topic of interest.
2. Record it on tape or in shorthand just as he gives it.
3. Play the tape or read the notes back to him.

Alternate Uses:

1. Repentance (using the tape recorder).
2. See yourself as others see you.

Lesson Application:

1. Man has found a way to keep a record of sound.
2. Surely God knows how to keep a record of our thoughts and actions.
3. We make a record each day in the minds of those with whom we associate.
4. Unlike a tape recording, however, we cannot erase the things that people remember about us—what we did, said, or enjoyed, etc.

Teaching with Objects   7

CHASTITY

Objective: To show that high standards are a protection to us.

Material Needed:

1. Two sticks of gum, with the wrappings removed from one

Presentation:

1. Pass around an unwrapped stick of gum for all to see and handle.
2. Follow it with another stick which has the wrappings on it.
3. Ask the class which they would prefer to chew? Why? Bring out the value of the packaging.

Lesson Application:

1. Our bodies can be passed around for everyone to handle.
2. Or, we can protect them with chastity.
3. Which body would you prefer for a mate?

8   *Teaching with Objects*

CHURCH STANDARDS

Objective: To show that if we do not stick to Church standards, our character suffers.

Material Needed:
1. Scotch tape
2. Sheet of paper

Presentation:
1. Stick the tape to the paper.
2. Now, tear it off and show the class the scar it left.

Lesson Application:
1. We need to stick to our Church standards.
2. If we ever let go, we leave a scar on our character.

Teaching with Objects   9

CONFORMITY

Objective: To show that we must conform to the Lord's will if we want to enter his kingdom.

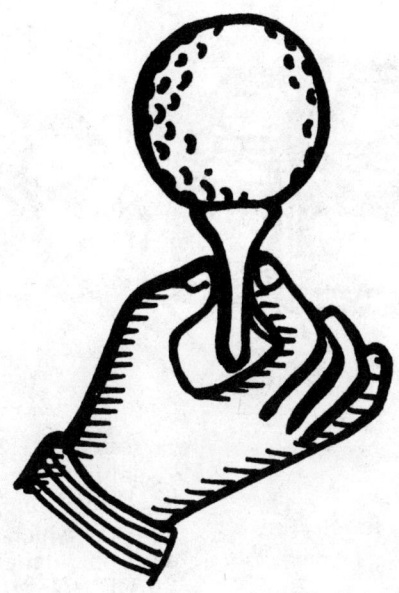

Material Needed:

1. A golf ball
2. A golf tee

Presentation:

1. Show the golf ball and tee to the class.
2. Place the ball on top of the tee and explain that the ball stays there because the tee conforms to the shape of the ball.
3. Now try to balance the ball on the pointed end of the tee, and explain that the ball will not rest here because the shapes of the two do not conform to each other.

Lesson Application:

1. If we want to be partners with God in his kingdom, we must conform to his plan and follow his commandments.

ETERNAL LIFE

Objective: To show that the right keys are necessary to gain eternal life.

Material Needed:

1. A jewelry box, with jewelry inside
2. A key ring with three miscellaneous keys, one labeled "wealth"; one, "social prestige"; and one, "power"
3. The key which opens the jewelry box, labeled "gospel of Christ" (place this key on the key ring also)

Presentation:

1. Show the jewelry box and keys to the class.
2. Show the label on one of the miscellaneous keys, and then try to open the jewelry box with it. Repeat the procedure with the other two miscellaneous keys.
3. Now, open the jewelry box with the key labeled "gospel of Christ."
4. Show the class the jewelry inside the box.

Lesson Application:

1. Emphasis is often placed on worldly things.
2. Eternal life and its accompanying blessings can only be obtained by living the gospel of Christ.

Teaching with Objects 11

ETERNAL MARRIAGE

Objective: To show that marriage as ordained by God is eternal.

Material Needed:

1. An engagement ring (may be obtained from a class member)

Presentation:

Allow all students to observe the beautiful ring, using appropriate comments about it, such as:

1. The ring is round, having no apparent beginning or ending.
2. The ring symbolizes the deepest love and devotion.
3. Its round shape symbolizes endless associations.

Lesson Application:

In analyzing the first marriage, we find the following:

1. The ceremony was performed by our Eternal Father at a time when Adam and Eve were not subject to "until death do you part." Therefore, marriage was intended to be for all eternity.
2. All that may have been lost through previous apostasy has been restored in these latter days through the Prophet Joseph Smith and his successors. (Refer to Doctrine & Covenants 76:132.)

EVOLUTION

Objective: To show that the earth and its inhabitants were created under divine direction and **not** through chance.

Material Needed:

1. Flashlight, disassembled
2. Plastic bag

Presentation:

1. Place in a plastic bag the disassembled flashlight.
2. Ask a member of the class to come forward and shake the bag until the flashlight falls back together. (Of course, this cannot be accomplished.)

Lesson Application

1. All of the elements to form the earth and its inhabitants were present.
2. The earth and its inhabitants were not created by chance or without direction any more than you can assemble this flashlight by merely shaking it in a bag.

Teaching with Objects   13

FAITH

Objective: To show that we need to keep our faith strong.

Material Needed:
1. A rubber band

Presentation:
1. Place one end of the rubber band around your little finger, and pull the other end upward through your clenched fist.
2. Slightly loosen your fist and let the band slowly disappear.

Lesson Application:
1. The rubber band represents faith, and the fist, a person and his mind.
2. As long as we keep our fist clenched, or our lives true to the gospel, then our faith remains stable and strong. But let our minds waver from the gospel and our faith dwindles away.

14 *Teaching with Objects*

FEELINGS

Objective: To show that feelings are transferred from one person to another by the way we act.

Material Needed:

1. Two or three delicate flowers
2. A vase of water

Presentation:

1. Blow on a delicate flower.
2. Have the class observe how it withers and curls up.
3. Place a withered flower in water and observe how it revives.

Lesson Application:

1. We radiate feelings by our actions.
2. Angry people can wither others.
3. We should be careful to radiate only feelings of love.

GOALS

Objective: To show that success is preceded by plans and preparation.

Material Needed:

1. Several one-inch-square pieces of paper
2. A paper cup

Presentation:

1. Place the cup on the floor, and from a waist height try to drop the squares into the cup.
2. Crumple one of the papers into a ball and try to drop it into the cup from the same height.

Lesson Application:

1. Without preparation, attempts to reach a goal meet resistance and are unsuccessful.
2. When attempts are directed by knowledge, testimony, and adequate preparation, however, the resistance is overcome and the goal is attained.

Teaching with Objects

GOALS

Objective: To show that we need to set goals in order to accomplish the things we would like.

Material Needed:
1. A straw
2. 2 balloons
3. 2 pieces of string or thread

Presentation:
1. Have a class member blow up one balloon and then let it go. It will fly around the room in all directions.
2. Now thread the string through the straw, leaving a foot or more at each end.
3. Tie a second balloon to the straw, placing the opening outwards so that it can be blown up.
4. Ask two students to hold on to the ends of the string.
5. Then blow up the balloon and let it go. It will force the straw down to one end of the string.

Lesson Application
1. Some people are like the first balloon in that they do not have definite goals or direction in life.
2. We must be like the second balloon and chart goals for ourselves which lead to significant accomplishments.

GODHEAD

Objective: To show that the Godhead consists of three distinct personages, united in purpose.

Material Needed:

1. A three-legged stool, preferably one whose legs screw in and out

Presentation:

1. Show the stool and call attention to the three legs.
2. Each leg is separate, yet they all work together to hold up the stool.
3. Screw out one of the legs, if possible, and demonstrate how the stool falls if one leg fails to perform its job.

Lesson Application:

1. The Godhead consists of three distinct personages.
2. All three are united in aim, will, and effort.

GOSPEL ENRICHMENT

Objective: To show that living the gospel enriches our lives.

Material Needed:
1. Salt shaker
2. Candle
3. Small plate or pie tin
4. Matches

Presentation:
1. Light the candle.
2. Stand the candle up on the plate, using wax drippings to hold it in place.
3. Sprinkle salt on the flame, thus making the flame flare up.

Lesson Application:
1. The candle represents life on earth.
2. When the gospel is added to our lives, it enriches them.

GOSSIP

Objective: To demonstrate the irreparable damage done by gossip.

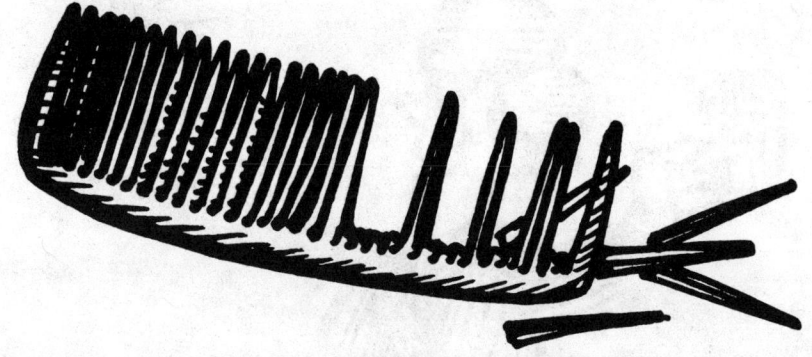

Material Needed:
1. An inexpensive comb

Presentation:
1. Show a comb and explain that it is made of many teeth.
2. Pass the comb around the group and have each student break out a tooth. Return the skeleton of the comb to the teacher.
3. The comb cannot be repaired or restored to its normal condition.

Lesson Application:
1. Our reputation is based upon all our acts.
2. Reputations may be destroyed through gossip.
3. Gossip, once released through idle conversation, never loses its sting and cannot be recalled.
4. Refer to James 3:5-10, 1:25.

HOLY GHOST

Objective: To show that the companionship of the Holy Ghost is dependent upon certain conditions and principles.

Material Needed:

1. Lights in the classroom

Presentation:

There is always light available IF:

1. The source is generating.
2. The house is properly wired.
3. The light bill is paid.
4. There is a bulb which can be illuminated by the power.

Lesson Application:

The influence of the Holy Ghost is present IF:

1. It is available—which it always is.
2. We have earned the right to receive it.
3. We keep God's commandments.
4. We are receptive to it. (List ways in which we can be receptive.)

Alternate Uses:

1. Omnipresence of the Spirit of the Lord—we just have to switch on our controls.
2. Authority—though the house is properly wired, no light is available until those with authority (power company) turn on the source.

Teaching with Objects 21

HONESTY

Objective: To show that a Church member's compliance with gospel principles helps to determine his success.

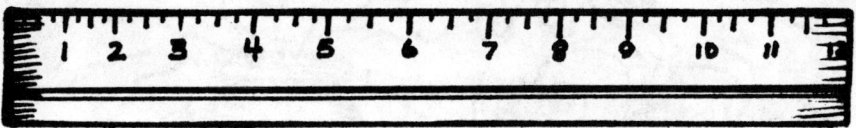

Material Needed:

1. A ruler in good condition
2. A ruler which has been (or can be in the demonstration) nicked and warped

Presentation:

1. Show a ruler to class and explain how each division represents a part of the ruler.
2. A ruler has a particular job.
3. The ruler is a means of measuring an object.
4. Show a ruler that is nicked, warped, etc.; hence, inaccurate for measuring and useless for the purposes for which it was made. OR, have a soft wood ruler and actually mar it in the demonstration.

Lesson Application:

1. A person's life is divided into many acts. Each act is a part of the whole life.
2. Each person has a purpose in life.
3. A person's success is measured by his individual accomplishments.
4. A person who becomes marred in life by dishonesty, etc., becomes less able to accomplish all that he was intended to.

22 Teaching with Objects

INFLUENCE

Objective: To show that we influence our surroundings.

Material Needed:

1. A small bottle of perfume
2. A bottle of ammonia

Presentation:

1. Open the bottle of perfume.
2. When it starts to permeate the room, open the bottle of ammonia.

Lesson Application:

1. We influence our surroundings, whether we be good (the perfume) or evil (the ammonia).

Teaching with Objects 23

JUDGMENT

Objective: To show that we should always be prepared to meet the Lord and his judgment.

Material Needed:

1. Stop watch

Presentation:

1. Have the group form a circle with their chairs.
2. Then have the group stand and each, using his own judgment, sit down when he thinks a minute is up. Use the stop watch to time them. Many will miss it.

Lesson Application:

1. If you can't predict when a minute is up, how can you expect to predict the time when you will meet your Maker?
2. Therefore, we all need to be ready for that time.

24   *Teaching with Objects*

KNOWLEDGE

Objective: To show that there is always room for more knowledge.

Material Needed:

1. Container
2. Rocks (enough to fill container)
3. Grain
4. Sand
5. Water

Presentation:

1. Fill container with as many rocks as possible. Point out that the container seems to be completely full.
2. Then pour grain over the rocks until completely full and it doesn't seem possible for anything more to fit into the container.
3. Repeat the procedure with sand and then water.

Lesson Application:

1. No matter how much knowledge a man has obtained, there is always room for more.

Teaching with Objects 25

LIGHT OF THE GOSPEL

Objective: To demonstrate how the gospel brightens our lives.

Material Needed:

1. Light socket or lamp
2. Three light bulbs—60 watts, 75 watts, and 100 watts. (A three-way bulb may be substituted if you have a three-way lamp)
3. A burned-out bulb

Presentation:

1. Show the burned-out bulb. It does not work because its wires are loose or disconnected.
2. Now turn on the 60-watt bulb.
3. Turn on the 75-watt bulb next. It is brighter than the 60-watt bulb.
4. Finally, turn on the 100-watt bulb. It is brighter than either the 60-watt or the 75-watt bulb.

Lesson Application:

1. The burned-out bulb represents a person without the light of the gospel in his life.
2. Once this person accepts the gospel, repents and is baptized, a light shines within him.
3. As he studies the scriptures, the light becomes brighter and more intense.
4. When he receives the priesthood and goes through the temple, the light becomes brighter still.
5. The Lord has told us to let the light of the gospel shine in our lives so that others seeing it will glorify him.

LIVING THE GOSPEL

Objective: To show that life seen through the gospel looks much brighter and more rewarding.

Material Needed:

1. Two class members who wear glasses

Presentation:

1. Ask someone who wears glasses to take them off and look at an object on the other side of the room.
2. Now have him put the glasses on. He can see clearly now.
3. Give the same person someone else's glasses and ask him if he can see as clearly with that pair as he can with his own.
4. When you get the correct prescription, you can see the best and be the happiest.

Lesson Application:

1. People without the gospel don't know what they are missing. They don't realize how much happier their life could be with the gospel.
2. A person may think he is happy without the gospel, but with it he sees the full meaning of life more clearly.
3. There are many gospels which profess to be the true one, but there is only one gospel prescribed by Christ that will help you to live your life at its fullest.

OBEDIENCE

Objective: To show that we must obey certain rules if we hope to obtain salvation.

Material Needed:
1. A combination lock

Presentation:
1. Show the combination lock to the class.
2. Ask several class members to try to open it.
3. After each has failed, open the lock, explaining that it is easy if you know the right combination.

Lesson Application:
1. We have been sent to earth in order to be tested.
2. The Lord has revealed the combination to be used in returning to his presence, and we need only to use it.

28 *Teaching with Objects*

PARTICIPATION

Objective: To show that we only get out of an activity what we put into it.

Material Needed:

1. Empty glass container
2. Pitcher of water

Presentation:

1. Show the empty container. How much water can we get out of the container?
2. Pour some water into the container. Now, how much water can we get out of the container?

Lesson Application:

1. If we put nothing into an activity, we can expect nothing out of it.
2. However, if we put effort into an activity, we reap benefits from it.

Teaching with Objects

PRESENTATION

Objective: To show that you must have an effective presentation if a talk. lesson, etc., is to be worthwhile.

Material Needed:

1. A nicely decorated cake
2. A wash cloth
3. A small pan of water
4. A towel

Presentation:

1. Show the cake to the class.
2. Walk up to a student or two and ask each if he would like a piece of cake.
3. When the student says he would, take a fistful of cake and hand it to him.
4. Naturally, the student will not want it then.
5. Clean up your hands.

Lesson Application:

1. Even though a talk, lesson, etc., has been thoroughly prepared, it must also be presented effectively or it will not fulfill its purpose.

PRIESTHOOD

Objective: To demonstrate to boys their responsibilities in accepting offices in the priesthood.

Material Needed:
1. A small ladder

Presentation:
1. Show the ladder to the class.
2. Point out that a ladder must be climbed rung by rung.
3. It would be difficult to reach the third rung if a foot slipped on the second.
4. The higher we climb, the greater the consequences if we fall.

Lesson Application:
1. A boy of twelve is given the priesthood.
2. As he masters the responsibilities of a deacon, he is advanced and given more responsibilities.
3. If he fails to master the responsibilities of a deacon, however, he is not advanced until he is ready.
4. The higher a man is advanced in the priesthood, the greater is his condemnation if he should fall into Satan's grasp.

Alternate Use:
1. This presentation may also be used to teach responsibility or to demonstrate the process by which one may grow in the gospel.

PROBLEMS

Objective: To show that problems can be either stumbling blocks or stepping-stones.

Material Needed:
1. A large sheet of paper labeled "problems"

Presentation:
1. Hold the paper up for the class to see.
2. This paper can be attacked in two ways:
   a. It can be met head-on and tackled all at once, which is difficult, or
   b. It can be tackled little by little (fold it accordion style) and overcome.

Lesson Application:
1. Our problems can be overcome by tackling them one at a time and using the experience from the last one to conquer the next one.

REPENTANCE

Objective: To show that repentance is real and practical.

Material needed:

1. Bar of Soap

Presentation:

1. Soap is a practical household necessity.
2. Soap is cleansing.
3. For physical cleanliness, soap must be applied frequently.

Lesson Application:

1. Repentance is a practical principle of the gospel.
2. Repentance is cleansing.
3. Spiritual cleanliness requires constant repentance.

Teaching with Objects   33

REPENTANCE

Objective: To show how repentance can remove our sins.

Material Needed:
1. Bottle, half full of water
2. Food coloring
3. Bleach

Presentation:
1. Show a bottle of clear water.
2. Then add a couple of drops of food coloring to the water.
3. Now pour bleach in the bottle, which will turn the water clear again.

Lesson Application:
1. We come to this earth sinless.
2. As we progress, each of us sins and it marks our souls.
3. However, through repentance our souls can become clean again.

34 Teaching with Objects

REPENTANCE

Objective: To show that repentance can erase our sins.

Material Needed:
1. A sheet of wax paper.
2. Black, wax shoe polish
3. Soft cloth

Presentation:
1. Spread shoe polish on the wax paper and allow to dry for a minute or two.
2. Wipe off the shoe polish until it can no longer be seen.

Alternate Use:
1. The gospel can protect us from the power of darkness as the wax protects the paper from the shoe polish.

Lesson Application:
1. The shoe polish represents sin.
2. No matter how dark it is, the Lord will wipe the slate clean when we repent.

Teaching with Objects 35

RESTRICTIONS

Objective: To show that restrictions are necessary in order for us to achieve. Sometimes the things that seem to hold us down are the things that hold us up.

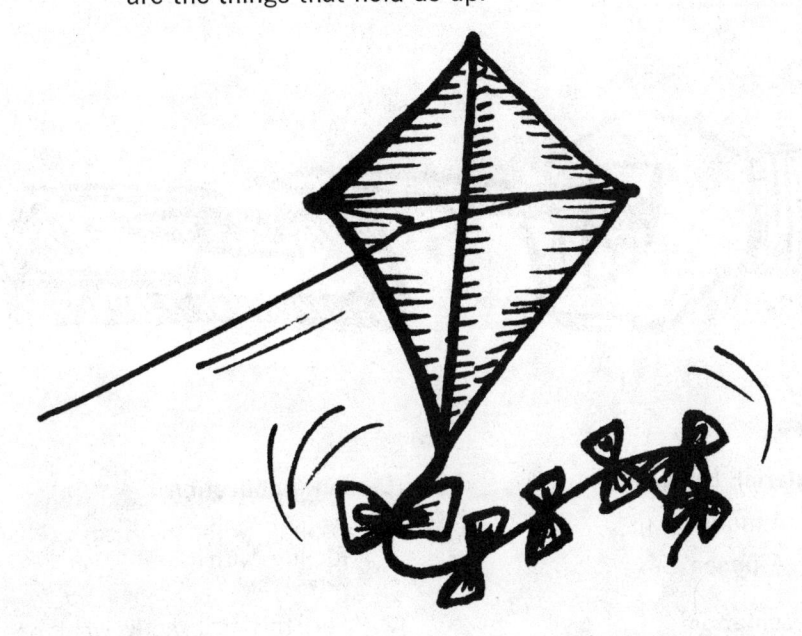

Material Needed:
1. Kite, with attached string
2. Playground, if practical

Presentation:
1. Fly the kite, and explain that the string holds the kite to the earth.
2. The string is also the means by which the kite is guided.
3. If the string were cut, the kite would fall.

Lesson Application:
1. The laws and ordinances of the gospel are meant to restrict some of our actions.
2. We are guided through commandments, revelation, and certain restrictions.
3. If we break the restraints by rejecting this guidance, we will fall and lose exaltation.

SATAN

Objective: To demonstrate that if we fool with Satan, we are going to get hurt.

Material Needed:

1. A mouse trap
2. A pencil

Presentation:

1. Bring the animal trap, all set, to the front of the class.
2. Take a pencil and spring the trap. The pencil will be crushed.
3. Set the trap again and ask for volunteers to spring it with their finger. No one will do so, because it would hurt.
4. The group will react as you touch the trigger lightly, or around the edges.

Lesson Application:

1. Fooling with the trap is like fooling with Satan. He is always "set."
2. Yet, this is exactly what people do when they pet, neck, or neglect the Word of Wisdom.
3. If you keep fooling around, one of these times you are going to set off the "trap," and when you do it is going to hurt.

SCRIPTURES

Objective: To show that the scriptures are often misread and misinterpreted.

Material Needed:
1. A card with "Paris in the the Spring" printed on it.
2. A card with "Once in a a Lifetime" printed on it
3. A card with "Bird in the the hand" printed on it.

Presentation:
1. Choose several people from the group and have them read aloud the three statements on the cards. Most people cannot read them as written. (Be sure you have printed them with the double word, as "Paris in **the the** Spring.")
2. Now point out the mistakes to the group.

Lesson Application:
1. We will never be able to attain the celestial kingdom if we do not read the scriptures and interpret them correctly.
2. We often make mistakes because we overlook simple things—things we think we already know.

SEEING ISN'T ALWAYS BELIEVING

Objective: To show that what appears to be right may be wrong.

Material Needed:
1. Glass of water
2. Straight stick

Presentation:
1. Place a straight stick in a glass of water.
2. Pull the stick out slowly; the bend in the stick changes.
3. Ask why the stick appears bent.

Lesson Application:
1. Things are not always as they seem; therefore, we should base decisions on true values rather than just on appearance.
2. Seeing is not enough; we need to apply other tests, too.

Alternate Presentations:
1. A picture of an Idaho potato bigger than a flat car may be used.
2. Some pictures that show the jackelope from Wyoming as being larger than an antelope may also be substituted.

SELF-DISCIPLINE

Objective: Self-discipline is difficult at first, but becomes easier with practice.

Material Needed:
1. A piece of chewing gum, preferably a big, hard piece of bubble gum

Presentation:
1. Put the whole piece of gum in your mouth at one time.
2. Begin to chew it laboriously, exaggerating a little so that it appears difficult to chew.
3. As the gum becomes more pliable, chew it with ease.

Lesson Application:
1. Self-discipline is more difficult to practice at the start.
2. With persistence, it becomes natural and easy.

SELF-IMPROVEMENT

Objective: To show that we must add work to wishing in order to become the kind of person we would like to be.

Material Needed:
1. Clay, or anything that can be treated as clay

Presentation:
1. Set a ball of clay on the table. Tell the class that looking at the ball of clay and wishing it would become a certain shape does not cause it to do so.
2. Pick up the clay and start molding it into the shape desired. Explain that through work it will eventually assume the desired shape.

Lesson Application:
1. If we stand around wishing we were a certain kind of person, we will never get our wish.
2. But if we work at it each day, we will eventually become the person of our dreams.

Alternate Use:
1. This lesson could be applied to show that work is necessary for achieving any goal in life.

Alternate Presentation:
1. Two approximately equal-sized stones may be used, one smooth and the other rough. The smooth, polished stone took work to make it pretty and desirable.

Teaching with Objects   41

SERVICE

Objective: To show that we should serve others.

Materials Needed:
1. Several candles
2. Matches

Presentation:
1. Light a candle.
2. Now, using the fire from this candle, light one or two other candles. Have the class observe that the flame flares up and is brightest when it is lighting the other candles.
3. By giving light to the other candles, has the first candle lost any of its flame?

Lesson Application:
1. Each of us has the ability within him to serve others.
2. When we are serving others, we feel the happiest.
3. It deprives us of nothing to serve others; on the contrary, it enriches our lives.

SHARING THE GOSPEL

Objective: To show why we should share the gospel with others.

Material Needed:

1. A bag of candy

Presentation:

1. Take a bag of candy and hold up one piece.
2. Then talk about how good it looks and how sweet it will taste.
3. Then say, "That's so good I want to share it with all of you," and pass out the candy to the rest of the group.

Lesson Application:

1. The gospel is the most prized possession we have.
2. Since it is important to our lives, shouldn't we want to share it with others to enrich their lives?

SIN CLOUDS THE VIEW

Objective: To show that the more we sin without repenting, the harder it is to repent.

Materials Needed:
1. Two blackboard erasers, filled with chalk dust

Presentation:
1. Tap the erasers together lightly to form a small cloud of dust.
2. Pound the erasers hard to form a dense cloud.

Lesson Application:
1. When we sin a little without repenting, it blurs our view of the right path a little, but we can still see our way back to our Father in heaven.
2. The more we sin, the more clouded our view becomes and the harder it is to repent.

SOCIAL PRESSURES

Objective: To show that social pressures become greater the more they are tolerated.

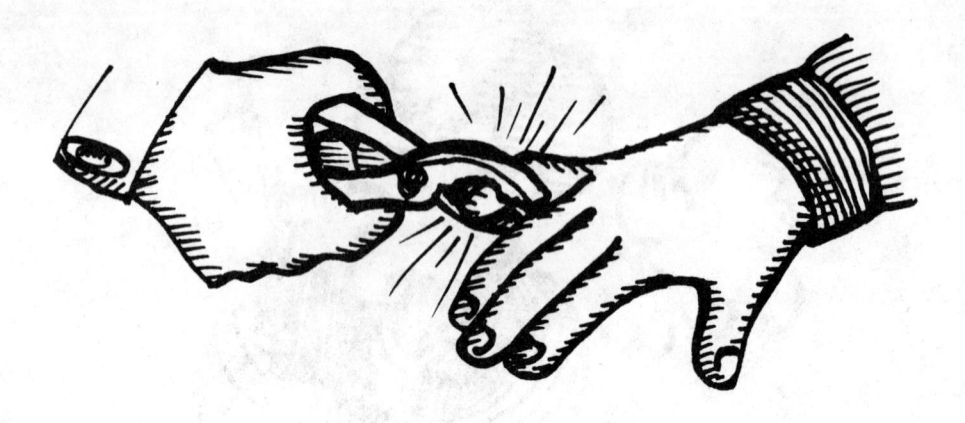

Material Needed:

1. A pair of pliers

Presentation:

1. Have a student come to the front of the class.
2. Attach a pair of pliers to his small finger.
3. Begin applying pressure gradually until he indicates the pressure is too great.

Lesson Application:

1. Just like the pliers, social pressure becomes greater the more it is tolerated.
2. We should learn to recognize social pressure when it begins to affect us. If the pressure is harmful, we should prevent it in time to protect our own character.

Teaching with Objects   45

SPIRIT OF THE LORD

Objective: To show that the Spirit of the Lord can guide us in our lives.

Material Needed:
1. Hard rubber comb
2. Table tennis ball
3. Piece of woolen cloth

Presentation:
1. Rub the comb vigorously with the woolen cloth, making the comb electrically charged.
2. Bring the comb near the table tennis ball. The ball will roll as the comb is moved.

Lesson Application:
1. When we listen to the still small voice we are being led by the Spirit of the Lord and can progress spiritually.

STRENGTH

Objective: It takes all the strength we can muster to withstand pressures and endure to the end.

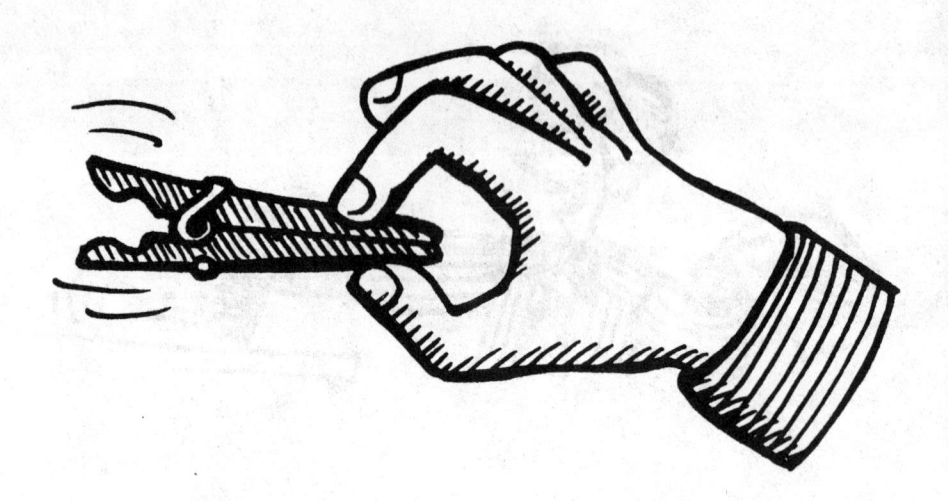

Material Needed:

1. Six clothespins
2. Six treats (such as candy)

Presentation:

1. Invite six students to the front of the class, both boys and girls.
2. Give them each a clothespin to be held between the forefinger and thumb with hand extended.
3. At the signal tell them to squeeze open the pin and keep it open for three minutes with no help from the other fingers.
4. To those who endure to the end, give a treat as a reward.

Lesson Application:

1. When our time comes, each of us is given a body.
2. We are given the gospel to direct our stay here on the earth.
3. The temptations and problems of earth life are sometimes hard to endure.
4. If we overcome Satan and endure to the end, our reward is the kingdom of heaven.

STRONG PHYSICAL BODY

Objective: To aid students in developing and strengthening their God-like bodies.

Material Needed:
1. Small candle
2. Glass

Presentation:
1. Light the candle and ask, What keeps it burning?
2. Place the glass over the candle and discuss why the flame is slowly extinguished.
3. Then ask what must be done to make the candle burn again.

Lesson Application:
1. The candle represents a healthy body.
2. What keeps it burning? Why must it be fed and kept active?
3. Too much rest smothers the cells (like the glass covering the flame), and fills the arteries with cholesterol.
4. List the evils that can cause our bodies to deteriorate.
5. List different ways we must keep active: physically, socially, spiritually, emotionally, and mentally.

Alternate Uses:
1. Like the candle flame. a testimony can be slowly stifled.

TALENTS

Objective: To show the necessity for constant use of our talents.

Material Needed:
1. Shiny piece of silverware
2. Tarnished piece of silverware
3. Silverware cleaner
4. Cloth

Presentation:
1. Take a piece of silverware and call attention to its brightness and beauty.
2. Show tarnished piece of silverware and explain that it became tarnished by not being used.
3. The more silverware is used, the brighter it becomes.
4. Demonstrate how cleaner can restore tarnished silverware to its original luster.

Lesson Application:
1. A person with talents is beautiful and of great service.
2. If talents are not used, they become dormant.
3. The more talents are used, the brighter they become.
4. Even though we have neglected our talents for a while, often we can reclaim them with use.
5. Talents may tarnish simply because we are unaware of them.

Alternate Uses:
1. Repentance—Even though we have sinned and our soul is tarnished, we can repent and be cleansed.

Teaching with Objects 49

TEAMWORK

Objective: To show that working together helps to accomplish a goal better and faster.

Material Needed:
1. A four-legged chair
2. Two to four persons

Presentation:
1. Have one person attempt to raise the chair over his head by holding the bottom of one chair leg with just one of his hands.
2. After a couple of people have tried this, have two to four individuals (depending on their age and strength) each lift a leg and show how easily the chair can be raised above the head level.

Lesson Application:
1. When we try to do hard tasks alone, we fail.
2. If we try to accomplish the same tasks by all working together, they are easily done.

Alternate Presentation:
1. Have any number of students try to lift the chair, one pulling one way and another the other. The chair will not be raised above the head level until all work together toward one common goal.

TEMPTATIONS

Objective: To show that we must be true and firm in the gospel to avoid falling into Satan's power.

Material Needed:

1. Pencil
2. Large flat object, such as a book or a board

Presentation:

1. Place the pencil in the middle of the board. Then, by holding onto each end of the board, tip it from side to side, seeing how close to the edge the pencil can roll without falling off.
2. Let the pencil fall off a couple of times.

Lesson Application:

1. The devil is constantly tempting us.
2. We don't know how much temptation we can take before we fall into his grasp, so we need to pursue a firm, straight course in the gospel and not stray from side to side.

Alternate Presentation:

1. Use a magnet and a nail, labeling the magnet "sin" and the nail "you." The magnet held at one end of the board will attract the rolling nail if the latter gets too close.

TESTIMONY

Objective: To show that we need a strong, solid testimony to withstand temptation.

Material Needed:
1. A heavy rock, labeled "testimony"
2. Inflated balloon, labeled "testimony"
3. Small board with a nail driven through it, labeled "temptation"

Presentation:
1. Show rock labeled "testimony." Point out that it has a few rough places.
2. Now show the balloon labeled "testimony." It seems smooth and good.
3. Using the nail on the board labeled "temptation," scratch the surface of the rock.
4. Then, pop the balloon with the "temptation" nail.

Lesson Application:
1. There are two kinds of testimonies: one is strong, while the other is weak and full of hot air.
2. We have to work hard to get a "rock" testimony. It comes by searching the scriptures, praying, and other things we have talked about.
3. The "balloon" testimony is easy to have. It is the "Brother........ said-it-was-true-so-I-believe-it-is-true" testimony. There is little inside of it and nothing to make it strong.
4. When confronted with temptation, the "rock" testimony suffers only a few scratches, but the same temptation bursts the "balloon" testimony.

TESTIMONY

Objective: To show that we obtain our testimony through our own experiences.

Material Needed:

1. A bottle of cologne or perfume

Presentation:

1. Have one or two class members smell the perfume and try to explain its fragrance to the others.

2. Now pass the bottle around and let each person smell the perfume.

Lesson Application:

1. Others can relate their spiritual experiences and guide us in obtaining a testimony.

2. But it is through our own experiences and feelings that we actually gain our testimones.

Teaching with Objects

THREE DEGREES OF GLORY

Objective: To show that we should strive to attain the celestial kingdom because it contains the greatest rewards.

Material Needed:

1. A ten-dollar bill
2. A one-dollar bill
3. A penny

Presentation:

1. Show the money to the class and ask several students which one they would rather have.
2. No doubt they will all say they would rather have the ten-dollar bill because it is the most valuable.

Lesson Application:

1. The Lord has given us the choice between the three degrees of glory. It is up to us which one we obtain.
2. Just as you would choose the ten-dollar bill because of its superior value, you should strive for the celestial kingdom because it has the most to offer.

Teaching with Objects

TIME FOR SEASONING

Objective: To show that this earthly life and its experiences prepare us for the celestial kingdom.

Material Needed:
1. A cucumber
2. A dill pickle
3. Salt
5. A watch
4. Vinegar

Presentation:
1. Place the materials in front of the class in the following order: cucumber, salt, vinegar, dill pickle, and watch.
2. Tell the story of the cucumber being turned into a pickle through the use of salt, vinegar, and time.

Lesson Application:
1. We come to this earth as a baby and receive a body.
2. Our experiences here and the temptations we overcome transform us so that we are prepared to live with our Father in heaven.

TITHING

Objective: To explain the meaning and purpose of tithing.

Material Needed:
1. Ten pennies

Presentation:

1. Give someone ten pennies.
2. Ask him to give one back to you.
3. Optional: label one blessing on the back of each penny. The one returned to the giver is labeled "wealth."

Lesson Application:

1. Our Heavenly Father gives us the things we have.
2. From our increase that he gives us, he requires that we return one-tenth for the building of his kingdom.
3. Through tithing we learn obedience.

56 Teaching with Objects

WEALTH

Objective: To point out that riches can be a curse or a blessing.

Material Needed:
1. A small piece of glass
2. A mirror

Presentation:
1. Ask a student to walk to the window and look out through a small piece of glass.
2. Have him describe what he sees.
3. Have a second student go to the window and look out through the mirror.
4. Have him describe what he sees.

Lesson Application:
1. What is the difference between a mirror and a plain piece of glass? (Just a little silver.)
2. When our soul is clear and uncoated, we look out and see our friends and the beauties of life.
3. If our soul becomes coated with silver, all we can see is ourselves.
4. The point should be made that, even as a mirror has many fine uses, so wealth can be used for good things.

WORD OF WISDOM

Objective: To show that tobacco is bad for our bodies.

Material Needed:
1. A goldfish
2. Two fishbowls or other containers of water
3. A cigarette

Presentation:
1. Show a healthy goldfish swimming in clean water. Note how frisky and normal the fish seems.
2. Hold up a cigarette for the class to see.
3. Unwrap the cigarette and crumble the tobacco into the water, stirring until uniformly distributed.
4. Ask the class to observe closely the fish's movements.
5. Note the increased activity of the fish due to the stimulus of the tobacco.
6. Gradually you will note the fish beginning to slow down, becoming sluggish in its movements.
7. The fish will eventually turn belly-side up. Then quickly remove it and put it in the clean water.

Lesson Application:
1. The fish represents a healthy person.
2. People often mistakenly think that tobacco as a stimulant helps them.
3. Sustained use of tobacco has been proven to be extremely dangerous and often results in death.

UNITY

Objective: To show that there is strength in unity.

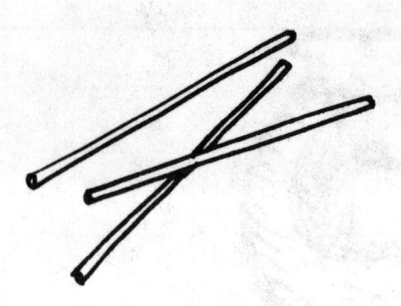

Material Needed:

1. Four small sticks about as big around as a pencil and about 12" long
2. About twelve to fifteen similar sticks tied together in a bundle

Presentation:

1. Ask someone if he thinks they could break one of the sticks in halves. Let someone do it. It should appear rather easy to do.
2. Ask if someone could hold two or three of the sticks together and break them all in halves. Let someone try it.
3. Point out how much more difficult it is to break two or three sticks than it is to break only one.
4. Ask if someone could take the bundle of sticks and break them in halves. Let someone try it.
5. Ask why it is almost impossible to break the bundle in halves. Emphasize that it is because the sticks are tightly tied together and thus lend their strength to each other. To break even one requires that all be broken.

Lesson Application:

1. Satan's temptations are powerful when we are alone in the world.
2. With our families around us, Satan must exert more pressure.
3. If we will stand firmly together as a Church and as children of God, Satan will have no power over us.